Alfred's Basic Piano Libr

MW00561984

Piano
Sight Reading Book
Level 1A

Gayle Kowalchyk • E. L. Lancaster

Sight reading is a basic skill and students who read fluently will be able to enjoy playing the piano for a life-time. Teachers have long recognized the value of sight reading in the development of the pianist. Many famous teachers have suggested that sight reading should be a part of the student's daily practice routine. Pianists who have good sight-reading skills are able to learn more music, since the time required for learning new repertoire is reduced. In addition, students who sight read regularly learn more about style characteristics of composers, improve memory (tactile, aural and kinetic) and improve their concentration.

Alfred's Basic Piano Library, Sight Reading Book, Level 1A, teaches sight reading in a systematic way by creating sight-reading exercises based on the same concepts that the student is studying in Alfred's Basic Piano Library, Lesson Book, Level 1A. Most of these exercises are based on intervals and patterns. Because sight reading involves more than just reading notes, this book includes rhythm sight-reading drills and improvisation exercises to develop tactile freedom on the keyboard. Exercises are short and the music is generally easier than the corresponding pages in the Lesson Book.

The books are coordinated page-by-page with the corresponding LESSON BOOK and assignments are ideally made according to the instructions in the upper right corner of each page of the SIGHT READING BOOK. It is best to wait until the indicated pages in the Lesson Book have been covered before the corre-sponding material in the Sight Reading Book is studied.

Realizing that material can only be used for sight reading one time, the authors suggest the following procedure for using the pages in this book:

1. The student should initially sight read the page for the teacher at the lesson when the page is assigned. This allows for discussion of patterns within the music and should take no more than five minutes of the lesson time.

2. The student plays the page only one time each day during the practice week. Each day the page should be a little easier.

3. The student should play the page straight through for the teacher at the next lesson, and discuss problems encountered in the performance.

ISBN 0-7390-0498-0
Illustrations by Beverly Lazor-Bahr

Use with Alfred's Basic Piano Library
LESSON BOOK 1A, page 9.

Rhythm

1. Clap the following rhythms, counting aloud.

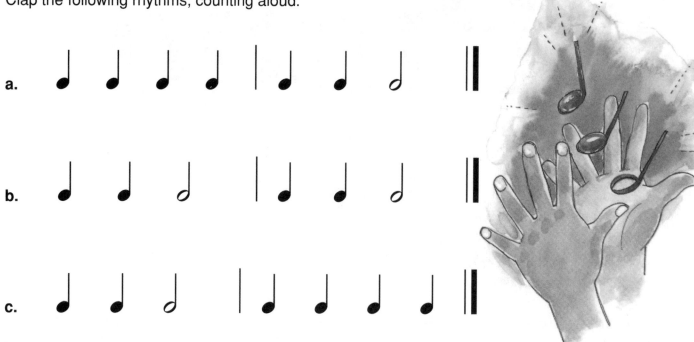

2. Create melodies in the given position using the rhythm pattern below.
   Begin and end each line with the given finger numbers.

3. Write the finger number above each right hand note and below each left hand note
   for your favorite melody.

POSITION

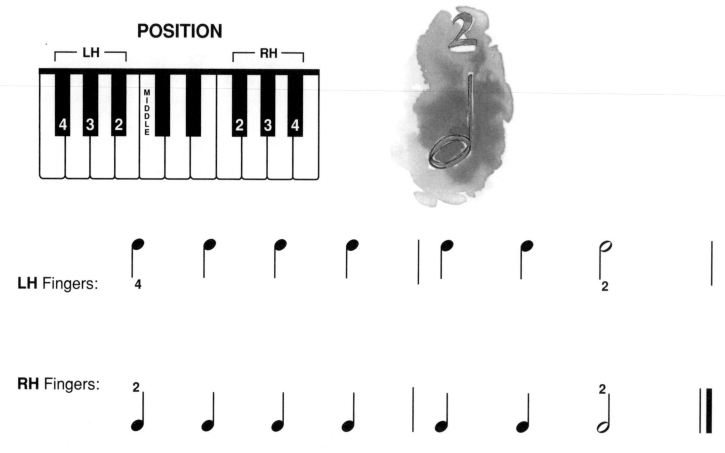

Reading

PRACTICE DIRECTIONS:

- Clap and count aloud.

- Play finger numbers in the air and count aloud.

- Play and count aloud slowly.

LEFT HAND POSITION

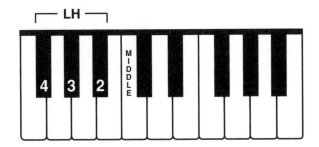

RIGHT HAND POSITION

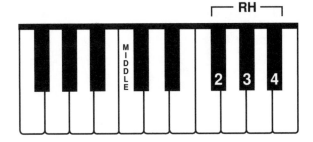

1.

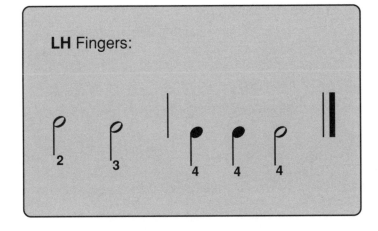

2.

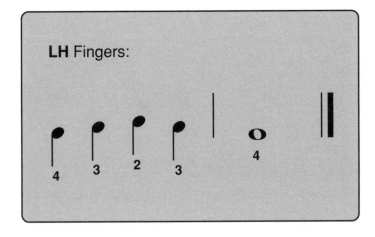

3.

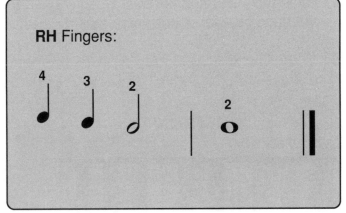

4.

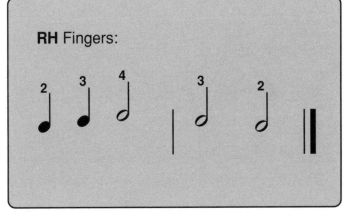

Use with page 13.

Rhythm

1. Clap the following rhythms, counting aloud.

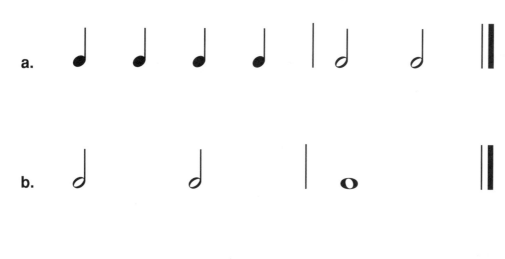

2. Create melodies in the given position using the rhythm pattern below. Begin and end each hand with the given finger numbers.

3. Write the finger number above each right hand note and below each left hand note for your favorite melody.

4. Write a dynamic sign (f or p) in the boxes.

POSITION

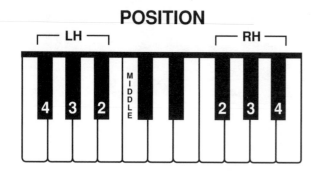

LH Fingers:

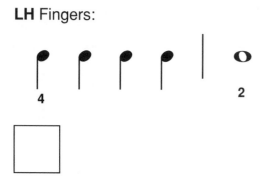

RH Fingers:

Reading

PRACTICE DIRECTIONS:

- Clap and count aloud.

- Play finger numbers in the air and count aloud.

- Play and count aloud slowly.

POSITION

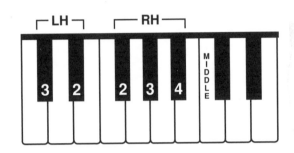

1.

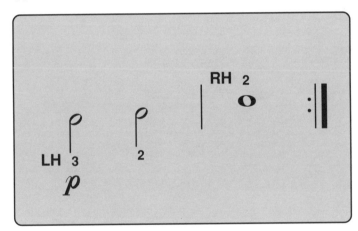

3.

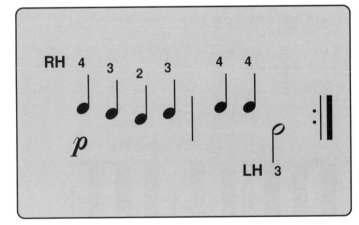

2.

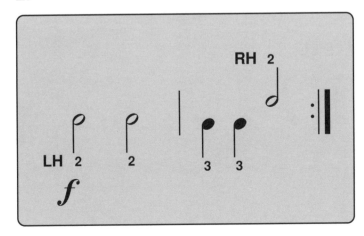

4.

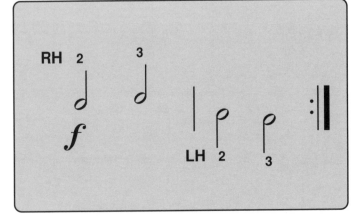

Rhythm

1. Clap the following rhythms, counting aloud.

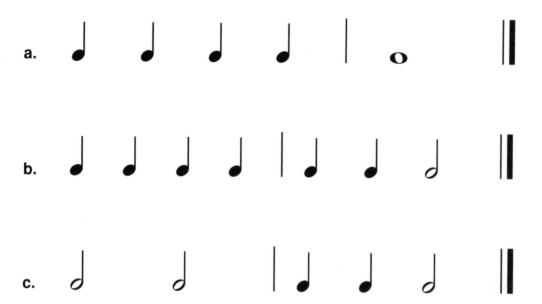

2. Create melodies in the given position using the rhythm pattern below.
   Begin and end each hand with the given finger numbers.

3. Write the finger number above each right hand note and below each
   left hand note for your favorite melody.

4. Write a dynamic sign (𝒇 or 𝒑) in the boxes.

POSITION

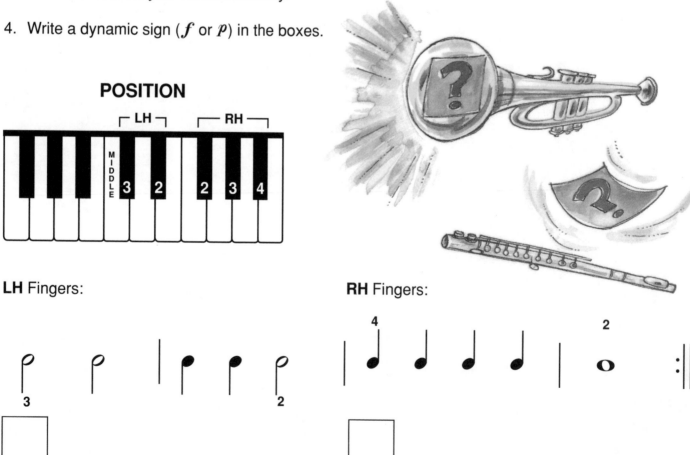

LH Fingers:

RH Fingers:

Reading

PRACTICE DIRECTIONS:

- Clap and count aloud.

- Play finger numbers in the air and count aloud.

- Play and count aloud slowly.

- Play and say the note names.

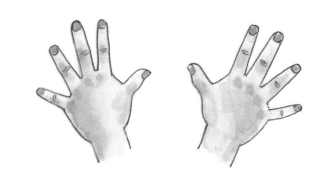

MIDDLE C POSITION

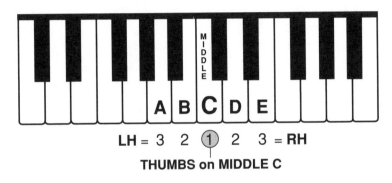

1.

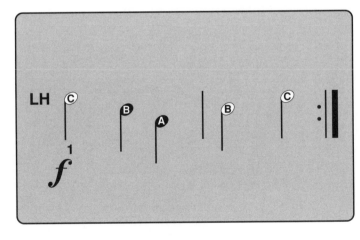

2.

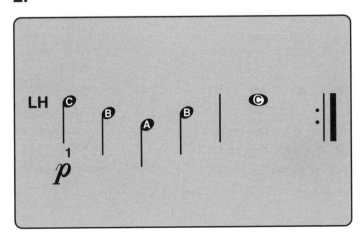

3.

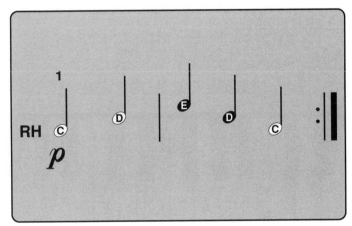

4.

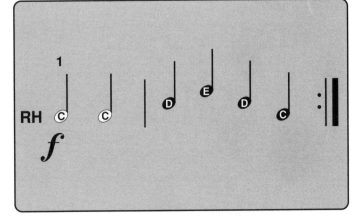

Use with page 21.

Rhythm

1. Clap the following rhythms, counting aloud.

a.

b.

c.

2. Create melodies in the given position using the rhythm pattern below. Begin and end each hand with the given finger numbers.

3. Write the finger number above each right hand note and below each left hand note for your favorite melody.

4. Write the note names on the line below each note for your favorite melody.

5. Write a dynamic sign (*f* or *p*) in the boxes.

MIDDLE C POSITION

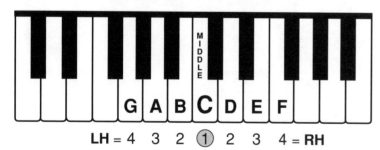

RH Fingers:

LH Fingers:

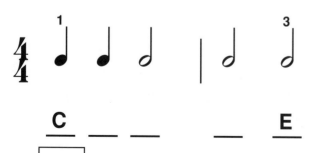

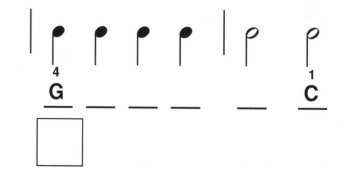

Reading

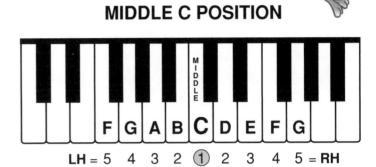

PRACTICE DIRECTIONS:

- Clap and count aloud.

- Play finger numbers in the air and count aloud.

- Play and count aloud slowly.

- Play and say the note names.

MIDDLE C POSITION

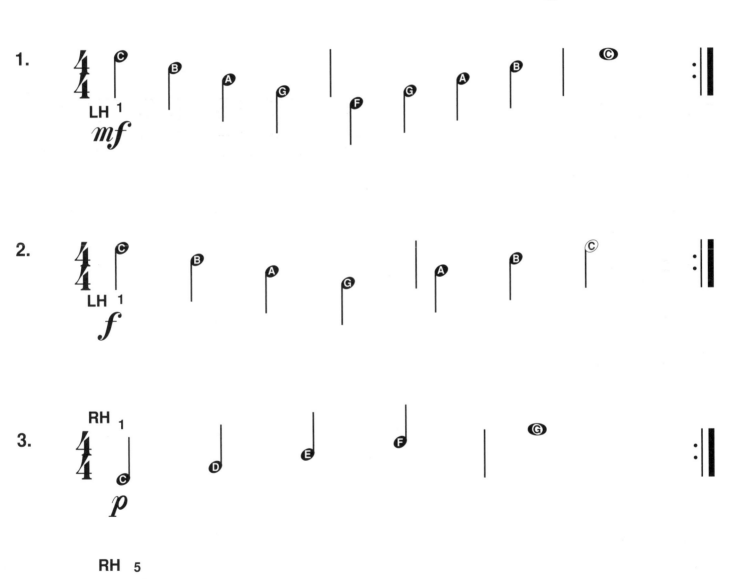

10

Use with page 24.

Rhythm

1. Clap the following rhythms, counting aloud.

 a.

 b.

 c.

C POSITION

2. Create melodies in the given position using the rhythm pattern below. Begin and end each hand with the given finger numbers.

3. Write the note name on the line below each note for your favorite melody.

4. Write a dynamic sign (*f* or *p*) in the boxes.

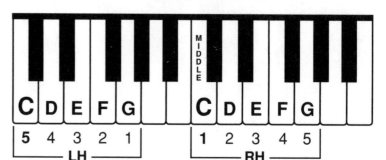

RH Fingers:

LH Fingers:

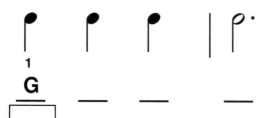  

Reading

PRACTICE DIRECTIONS:

- Clap and count aloud.

- Play finger numbers in the air and count aloud.

- Play and count aloud slowly.

- Play and say the note names.

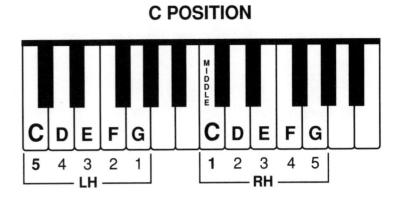

C POSITION

1. $\frac{3}{4}$ **F** **E** **D** **C.** :||
   LH **2**
   mf

2. $\frac{3}{4}$ **G** **F** **E** **G.** :||
   LH **1**
   f

3. $\frac{3}{4}$ **E** **E** **D** **C.** :||
   LH **3**
   p

4. RH **1**
   $\frac{3}{4}$ **C** **D** **E** **C.** :||
   p

5. RH **2**
   $\frac{3}{4}$ **D** **E** **F** **G.** :||
   f

6. RH **4**
   $\frac{3}{4}$ **F** **G** **F** **E.** :||
   mf

Use with page 26.

Rhythm

1. Clap the following rhythms, counting aloud.

a.

b.

c.

C POSITION

2. Create melodies in the given position using the rhythm pattern below. Begin and end with the given finger numbers.

3. Write the note name on the line below each note for your favorite melody.

4. Write a dynamic sign (f or p) in the boxes.

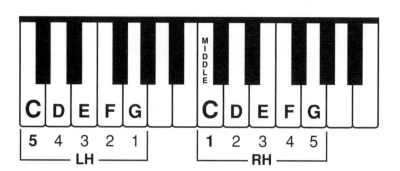

RH Fingers:

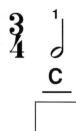

LH Fingers:

Reading

PRACTICE DIRECTIONS:

- Clap and count aloud.

- Play finger numbers in the air and count aloud.

- Play and count aloud slowly.

- Play and say the note names.

C POSITION

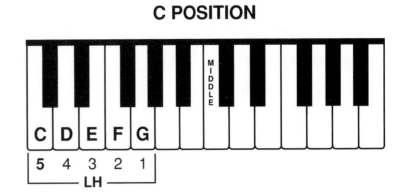

1.

2.

3.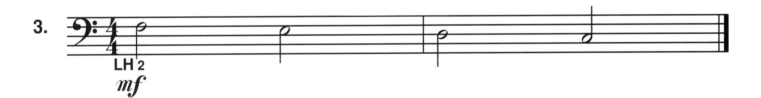

4.

5.

6.

14

Use with page 31.

Reading

PRACTICE DIRECTIONS:

- Clap and count aloud.
- Play finger numbers in the air and count aloud.
- Play and count aloud slowly.
- Play and say the note names.

C POSITION

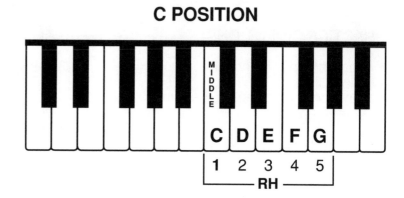

1.

2.

3.

4.

5.

6.

Use with page 35.

Rhythm

1. Clap the following rhythms, counting aloud.

a.

b.

c.

2. Create a melody in C Position using the rhythm pattern below.
   Begin and end with the given notes in each hand.

3. Write the notes for your melody on the staff.

4. Write a dynamic sign (*f* or *mf*) in the boxes.

5. Draw a slur to connect the first and last notes of the right hand.

6. Draw a slur to connect the first and last notes of the left hand.

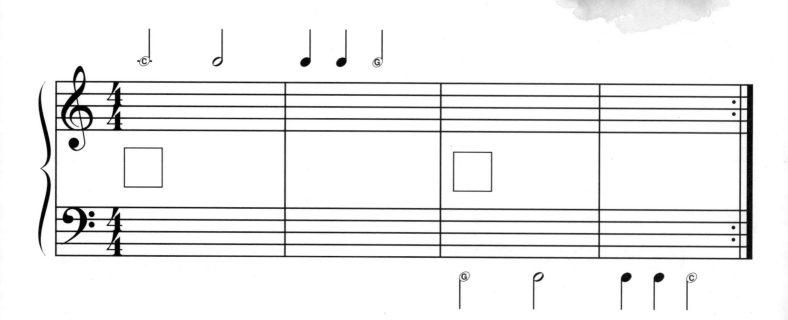

Reading 2nds in C Position

1. Play the following intervals from C Position using the correct fingers.

a.

b.

c.

d.

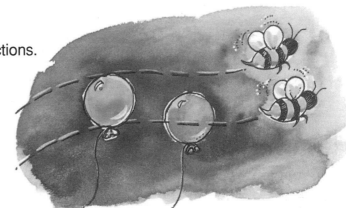

2. Play the following melodies using the practice directions.

   - Clap and count aloud.
   - Play finger numbers in the air and count aloud.
   - Play and count aloud slowly.
   - Play and say the note names.

a.

b.

c.

d.

18

Reading 3rds in C Position

1. Play the following intervals from C Position using the correct fingers.

a.  **b.** 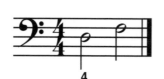 **c.**  **d.**

2. Play the following melodies using the practice directions.

   • Clap and count aloud.

   • Play finger numbers in the air and count aloud.

   • Play and count aloud slowly.

   • Play and say the note names.

a.

b.

c.

d.

Rhythm

1. Clap the following rhythms, counting aloud.

a.

b.

c.

2. Create a piece with only harmonic 2nds and 3rds in C Position using the rhythm pattern below. Use the thumb in each harmonic interval.

3. Write a dynamic sign (*f* or *mf*) in the boxes.

RH Fingers:

LH Fingers:

Use with page 43.

Reading in C Position

1. Play the following harmonic and melodic intervals from C Position using the correct fingers.

a.

b.

c.

d.

2. Play the following melodies using the practice directions.

    • Clap and count aloud.

    • Play finger numbers in the air
      and count aloud.

    • Play and count aloud slowly.

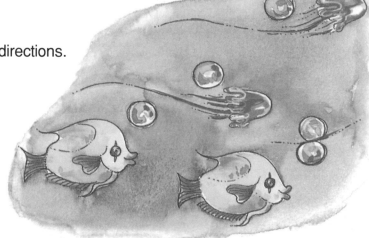

a.

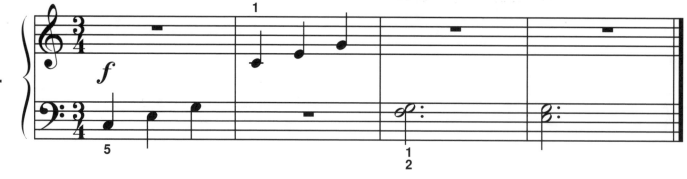

b.

Reading 4ths in C Position

1. Play the following melodic intervals from C Position using the correct fingers.

a.

b.

c.

d.

2. Play the following melodies using the practice directions.

    • Clap and count aloud.

    • Play finger numbers in the air and count aloud.

    • Play and count aloud slowly.

    • Play and say the note names.

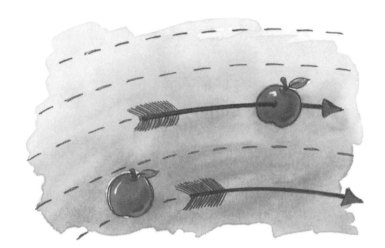

a.

b.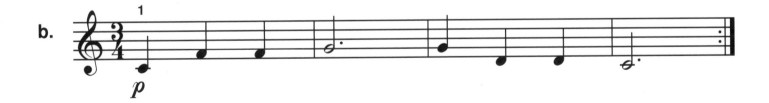

c.

d.

Use with page 47.

Rhythm

1. Clap the following rhythms, counting aloud.

2. Create a piece with only harmonic 2nds, 3rds and 4ths in C Position using the rhythm pattern below. Use the thumb in each harmonic interval.

3. Write a dynamic sign (f or p) in the boxes.

RH Fingers:

LH Fingers:

Reading 5ths in C Position

1. Play the following melodic intervals from C Position using the correct fingers.

a.    **b.** 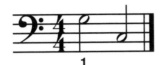   **c.** 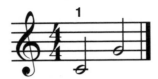   **d.**

2. Play the following melodies using the practice directions.

- Clap and count aloud.
- Play finger numbers in the air and count aloud.
- Play and count aloud slowly.
- Play and say the note names.

a.

b.

c.

d.

Use with page 51.

Reading in G Position

PRACTICE DIRECTIONS:
- Clap and count aloud.
- Play finger numbers in the air and count aloud.
- Play and count aloud slowly.
- Play and say the note names.

Rhythm

1. Clap the following rhythms, counting aloud.

a.

b.

c.

2. Create a piece with only harmonic 2nds, 3rds, 4ths and 5ths in G Position using the rhythm pattern below. Use the thumb in each harmonic interval.

3. Write a dynamic sign (*mf* or *p*) in the boxes.

RH Fingers:

LH Fingers:

Rhythm/Reading

Use with page 54.

1. Clap the following rhythms, counting aloud.

a.

b.

c.

2. Play the following harmonic and melodic intervals from G Position using the correct fingers.

a.

b.

c.

d.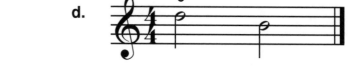

e.

f.

Reading with Sharps

1. Play the following intervals with sharps using the given beginning finger.

a.  **b.**  **c.**  **d.**

2. Play the following melodies using the practice directions.

   • Clap and count aloud.

   • Play finger numbers in the air and count aloud.

   • Play and count aloud slowly.

   • Play and say the note names.

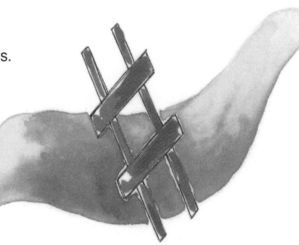

a.

b.

c.

d.

28

Use with page 56.

Reading with Flats

1. Play the following intervals with flats using the given beginning finger.

a.  **b.** 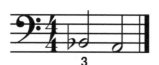 **c.** 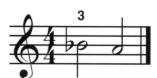 **d.**

2. Play the following melodies using the practice directions.

   • Clap and count aloud.

   • Play finger numbers in the air and count aloud.

   • Play and count aloud slowly.

   • Play and say the note names.

a.

b.

c.

d.

Rhythm

1. Clap the following rhythms, counting aloud.

2. Create a piece in G Position using the rhythm pattern below.
   Use a flat (♭) for each B. Begin and end with the given notes.

3. Write the notes for your melody on the staff.

4. Write a dynamic sign (*f* or *p*) in the box.

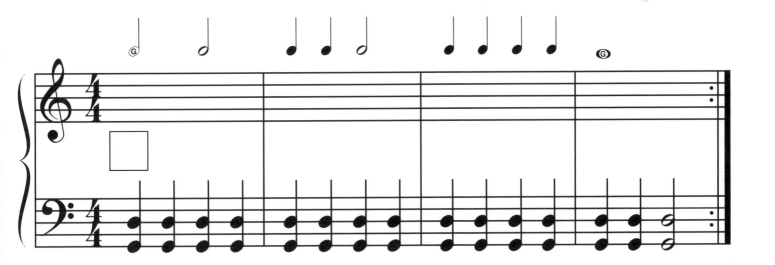

Use with page 58.

Reading

PRACTICE DIRECTIONS:

- Clap and count aloud.

- Play finger numbers in the air and count aloud.

- Play and count aloud slowly.

- Play and say the note names.

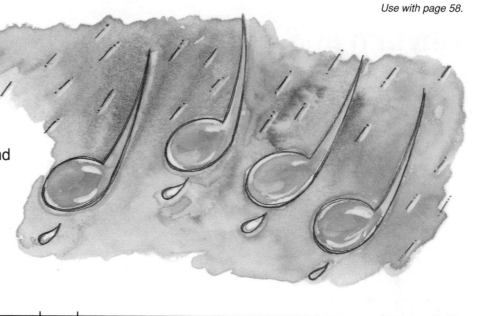

1.

2.

3.

4.

Reading in G Position

PRACTICE DIRECTIONS:

• Clap and count aloud.

• Play finger numbers in the air and count aloud.

• Play and count aloud slowly.

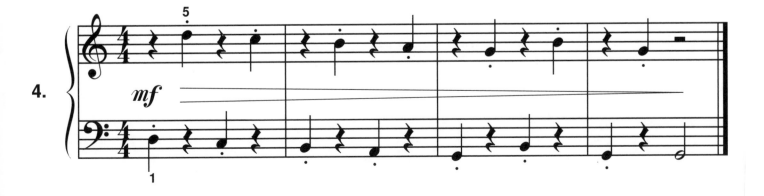

Use with pages 60–61.

Reading in C Position

PRACTICE DIRECTIONS:

• Clap and count aloud.

• Play finger numbers in the air and count aloud.

• Play and count aloud slowly.

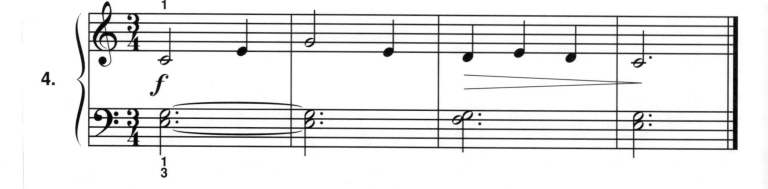